Empower Her

The Money Mindset Journal

ISBN: 978-1-7326800-1-2

Hello Lovelies

Welcome to the

Empower Her: Money Mindset Journal

This journal is designed to help you shift your mindset into one of **wealth, worth, and prosperity** — not by chasing, but by becoming.

Since leaving my Wall Street career in 2019 I've been on deep journey of introspection and self-discovery in pursuit of purpose. While I thought that I was on a purely spiritual path — letting go of materialism — I realized something very profound:

There is nothing more spiritual than the natural laws of abundance.

It is our birthright.

Yet we live in a system that deceives us into believing otherwise. It captures our thoughts, shapes our beliefs — to ultimately control our behaviors. Money, which is fundamental to our lives, has been turned into a **primary lever of control.**

Money has been made intentionally opaque, mysterious, and intimidating. But money is not the enemy. It is an instrument of expansion — one that should amplify our experiences, not restrict them.

The challenge is that most of us have been conditioned to live with **scarcity mindset,** believing that having "enough" is *always* just out of reach. We let money dictate our choices suppress our self-worth and limit our possibilities.

These patterns are rooted in ***money wounds*** *— emotional imprints formed by past experiences and inherited beliefs.*

This journal is your invitation to heal your relationship with money, rebuild self-trust and open yourself to new opportunities that can change the entire trajectory of your life.

That is my deepest intention in creating this journal — to guide you back to the truth of who you are.

I can't wait to hear about your transformation and see how this work helps you live the life you were always meant and fully deserve, to live.

With love and sincerity,

Tamara

INTRODUCTION

Your New Relationship with Abundance

If the mere thought of money makes you uneasy — this journal is for you.

If talking about money makes you uncomfortable — this journal is for you.

If asking for more money makes you want to hurl — this journal is *definitely* for you.

Creating wealth isn't about hustle. It's an energetic identity shift. It's about embodying the very wealth you desire and aligning with its frequency. It's remembering that abundance isn't something you chase — it's something you *allow.*

For many women, that shift requires unraveling old beliefs that have kept prosperity out of reach. It means releasing the quiet conditioning that taught you that wealth is for someone else — not you.

So, consider this your permission slip — the one you've always yearned for but were too afraid to give yourself.

That stops right here. Right now.

In these pages, you'll explore your earliest memories about money, confront the fear, the pain and the experiences that left scars. You'll unlearn self-silencing patterns and rewire the beliefs that have quietly dictated your financial reality.

You'll begin to see how your thoughts, emotions, and energy shape your ability to attract — not just money, but opportunities, possibilities, and even miracles.

And then — day by day — you'll shift your vibration to the frequency where wealth and abundance already exist as your natural state.

This journal is your sacred space to recondition your relationship with prosperity and align with the flow that has always been waiting for you. Healing your wounds isn't about guilt, blame, or shame — it's about **compassion, forgiveness, and the gentle release of the pain you've been carrying.**

Once that energy clears, you'll feel inspired by the power of possibility. You'll step into — and fully embody — a new emotional frequency that lifts you to a higher state of awareness, one that only comes from remembering who you truly are:

A woman who was always meant to prosper.

Let's begin.

HOW TO USE THIS JOURNAL

This is more than a journal — it's a journey to rewrite your money story, rewire your beliefs, and reconnect with your natural state of abundance.

Each section is designed to bring you deeper into alignment with wealth, ease and self-trust.

This isn't about manifesting from wishful thinking; it's about becoming the kind of woman who naturally attracts prosperity — because she already embodies it.

Here's how to make the most of your practice:

- **Commit to the Journey.**

  Your transformation will unfold in its own divine timing. Some pages will call for deep reflection, while others will flow easily. This isn't a race and there is no deadline.

  For some, this process will take 60 days. For others, it may take 6 months — or it may become a lifelong practice of returning home to yourself.

  Once you embark on this journey, it never truly ends. All I ask is that you **commit to doing the work.**

  Set aside a few moments each day to be with yourself. And if there are days you simply don't feel like doing the work, give yourself grace. This is as much about aligning your **body, mind and spirit** — and harnessing the power of that congruence.

  Energy responds to intention, not discipline.

► **Create Your Sacred Space**

Choose a quiet corner, light a candle, or play soft music — whatever helps you feel grounded and connected. This is your space to listen inwardly. Approach it as a daily ritual of remembering your worth.

► **Follow the Daily Flow**

Each day includes:

- **A reflection** — a thought or teaching to guide your mindset
- **An affirmation** — to anchor the frequency of abundance
- **A journal prompt** — to explore your beliefs and emotions
- **Space to write** — for your insights, reflections, and revelations

Let your words flow freely. There's no "right" way to do this work. Some days, you may write paragraphs. Others, a single sentence might hold your truth.

Both are perfect.

► **Revisit Your Entries**

From time to time, pause and reread what you wrote. Notice the patterns, shifts, and breakthroughs. Awareness is the first sign of transformation.

You're not just recording thoughts — you're witnessing your evolution.

► Feel Your Feelings

There will be moments in this journal that touch something tender — a memory, a wound, or a truth you've avoided.

You may feel resistance. You may cry. Let it come.

Don't suppress what surfaces. Allow yourself to feel it fully.

Tears are medicine. Crying is cathartic — it clears emotional energy and makes space for transformation.

This work isn't easy. Your breakthrough is on the other side of that discomfort.

When emotions arise, breathe through them. Forgive what needs forgiving — including yourself.

Breathe. Forgive. Continue.

► Becoming

By the end of this journey, you will emerge as a new version of yourself — lighter, clearer, and more deeply connected to your truth.

Money will no longer feel heavy or hard. It will become an effortless extension of your self-expression — a reflection of who you've always been becoming.

► **Remember**

The true magic of this journal isn't in the pages — it's in the presence you bring to them.

Your awareness, your intention and your courage to look within are what transform insight into embodiment.

So, take a deep breath, open your heart, and let's begin the sacred journey of remembering your natural state of wealth, worth, and abundance.

Section One

MONEY IS ENERGY

MONEY IS ENERGY

Money is energy. It flows, expands, contracts and responds to the beliefs, emotions and frequency of the person interacting with it.

It has no fixed form. Coins and notes are merely vessels for an energy as boundless as the universe itself.

When you chase money, it will elude you. Prosperity arrives when you stop chasing and start attracting—when you align with the frequency of its resonance.

The energy of money responds to resonant hearts, not to grasping hands.

Money just is.

It's not emotional. It's neutral.

You are the emotional charge.

- Energy is created through your thoughts.
- Energy is created through your words.
- Energy is created through your imagination.
- Energy is created through your intention.

Your mind broadcasts a frequency into the universe every moment of every day. These transmissions — your thoughts, feelings and beliefs about money create a field of energy that either attracts or repels prosperity.

When you dwell upon lack you emanate the frequency of scarcity.

When you focus on abundance with unwavering faith, you broadcast the signal of prosperity.

The universe in its infinite wisdom responds not only to your words alone but to the *feelings* behind them.

We begin here — not with spreadsheets, budgets, or strategies — but with **energy.**

Exercise One

Your Current Money Frequency

Close your eyes. Take a slow, deep breath. Place one hand on your heart and one on your belly. Think about *money* — not the bill, not the budget, not the goal — but the **concept of money itself**.

Then ask yourself:

"What emotion lives in my body when I think of money?"

Is it…

- Tension
- Fear
- Hope
- Lack
- Excitement
- Overwhelm
- Numbness
- Detachment
- Possibility

Write it here — without editing, just honesty:

What I FEEL when I think about money:

Now, ask yourself: **"Where do I feel that emotion in my body?"**

Select one:

- ☐ Chest
- ☐ Throat
- ☐ Stomach
- ☐ Solar plexus
- ☐ Shoulders
- ☐ Jaw
- ☐ Other________________________________

Journal what the sensation feels like:

This emotional imprint is your current frequency.
We cannot shift what we will not witness.

Exercise Two

How Do I Think About Money?

Complete the sentence:

"Money is..."

Complete the sentence:

"Money takes away..."

Complete the sentence:

"Money takes away..."

These meanings reveal the programs shaping your relationship with receiving.

JOURNAL PROMPTS

When it comes to money — what am I afraid of?

What is my deepest intention for wealth, abundance, and prosperity — what do you want?

If money is energy, what does my frequency radiate? How are others perceiving my financial frequency?

EMBODIMENT STEP

Begin to raise your awareness about your financial frequency and begin to embody your desired wealth.

Allow yourself to walk into shops that carry expensive items. Act like you belong.

Window shopping will help you visualize the reality you desire. Imagine buying what you want without consideration of price.

How does this make you feel? When you come home journal about the experience.

AFFIRMATION

I am a wealthy woman. Money flows to me with grace and ease.

SECTION 1 CLOSING

Money is energy.

To attract it, I must align my frequency to it.

Section Two

THE SPELL OF SCARCITY

THE SPELL OF SCARCITY

Scarcity is not only a financial condition. **It's a spell.**

A spell cast through language, modeled through behavior, and reinforced through culture, family, and society.

The beliefs you carry about money are not always your own. They're inherited — handed down through family lineage.

That's why it is often said that poverty is generational — not because money doesn't exist in the family...but because *beliefs* are programmed into the minds of one generation to another.

The universe knows no scarcity. Look at the night sky — The endless stars, the limitless grains of sand, the uncountable blades of grass. **Abundance is the natural state of existence.**

Your inherited beliefs about money form invisible chains binding you to pattern that do not serve your highest good.

The notion that you must choose between spiritual richness and material abundance are not your truths — but borrowed burdens.

And yet, many of us were taught:

- "Money doesn't grow on trees."
- "Money is the root of all evil."
- "People like us don't have that."

Or we absorbed a general disdain or jealousy for "rich people."

When you inherit beliefs like these, you unconsciously inherit the limits that come with them. This section is where you begin to return what was never yours to carry.

Exercise One

The Borrowed Garment

Scarcity is not your natural state. It is a borrowed garment worn so long you've forgotten it isn't your own. It's time to return what was never truly yours.

Step 1 — Name the Beliefs

Write down five of the strongest scarcity beliefs that echoed through your family line.

My inherited scarcity beliefs:

1. ____________________

2. ____________________

3. ____________________

4. ____________________

5. ____________________

Step 2 — Name the Source

Where did each belief come from — your mother, father, teacher, culture, or religion?

Step 3 — Break the Spell

Now, beside each belief, ask yourself:

Are these beliefs actually true?

Find evidence that they aren't. Redefine your new truths.

JOURNAL PROMPTS

What did you learn about "asking" in your family?

When did you first feel that you were asking for "too much" for wanting more?

How was money thought of in your family?

EMBODIMENT STEP

For the next 48 hours, notice moments when you fall back on phrases that were repeated in your family.

Each time it happens, pause and reframe them.

Note how often it happens.

AFFIRMATION

I release the beliefs that were never mine. Scarcity was never mine to keep.

SECTION 2 CLOSING

You are not bound by the limits of your lineage.

The spell of scarcity breaks the moment you choose abundance as your truth.

Section Three

MONEY AS A MIRROR

MONEY AS A MIRROR

Money is a mirror that reflects with perfect accuracy the image you hold within.

When you judge the wealth of others, you judge yourself. When you resent others for having more, you are really resenting yourself.

Your relationship with money echoes your relationship with yourself.

Abundance doesn't flow from external circumstances; it flows from **internal alignment**. Money responds to your inner state.

When you approach life with an open heart and believe in the endless nature of **prosperity**, the universe mirrors your expectation.

When you clutch at wealth with desperate hands, you create resistance in the very channel through which it flows.

Exercise One

Meeting Money

Picture yourself sitting at a table in a café. Money walks in and sits across from you.

Describe the scene in detail:

1. What does Money look like?

2. How is it dressed?

3. What is the expression on its face?

4. Where does it sit in relation to you — close, distant, hesitant?

5. Does Money speak to you? If so, what does it say?

This visualization reveals your current relationship with money. Notice the tone of the interaction — is there warmth, tension, avoidance, or curiosity? There's no wrong answer. Only truth.

Exercise Two

Reflection in Action

How are your current emotions about money manifesting in your external world?

Look at your bank account, your spending habits, your generosity, and your fears.

What do they reflect about your inner beliefs?

JOURNAL PROMPTS

What emotions come up when I check my bank account?

When have I felt judged or ashamed about money?

How do I speak about money when I'm with others?

If money were a mirror, what truth is it reflecting back to me right now?

DEEP EXERCISE

Write a Letter to Money

Write a letter to money expressing how you feel about it today. Be honest—vent, confess, appreciate, ask. It's about acknowledging the relationship — with honesty and heart.

"Dear Money, ..."

AFFIRMATION

I choose to expand my self-image and embody greater worth.

As my self-value rises, my bank account reflects that shift.

PAUSE + INTEGRATE

Honor what surfaced. Place a hand on your heart. Inhale, exhale.

Section Four

YOUR MONEY STORY

YOUR MONEY STORY

Your money story is a narrative you've absorbed over your lifetime — through your upbringing, media, culture, and personal experiences.

From a young age, many women internalize a story of limitation.
That they should be grateful for whatever they're offered.
That asking for more is dangerous.
That money is hard to get — and even harder to keep.

Without realizing it, you may find yourself repeating a story that was never yours to begin with. Maybe you learned that wanting more made you *selfish*.

Maybe you watched women in your family stretch every dollar while men made the financial decisions. Maybe you were praised for being *low-maintenance*, *selfless*, or *the helper* — and now that same conditioning shows up as undercharging, overworking, or people-pleasing.

Your money story has been written by many authors.
But now, it's your turn to pick up the pen.

Exercise One

The Money Timeline

Draw a mental timeline of your life in decades:

Childhood → Teens → Early Career → Now.

For each stage, reflect:

Childhood: What did I learn about money from my caregivers?

Teens: How did I first start earning, spending, or saving?

Early Career: What did I believe I "had to do" to be successful?

Now: How do those beliefs still show up in how I earn, ask, or spend?

Write down the moments that stand out — conversations, experiences, or emotions that shaped your view of money.

Exercise Two

Who Gets to Have Money?

Every family, culture, and community has an unspoken hierarchy around money — who "gets" to have it, who doesn't, and what it says about you if you do.

1. **Who did you see as "allowed" to have wealth growing up?**
2. **What kind of people were considered "rich," and how were they described?**
3. **What messages did you receive about ambition, luxury, and success?**

Write your reflections here:

Then ask yourself:

What beliefs have I subconsciously accepted as truth about who I am "allowed" to become?

JOURNAL PROMPTS

What role did money play in my home growing up — tension, secrecy, hope, pride?

How did I learn to measure my value — through effort, perfection, or performance?

How does that early story still shape how I negotiate, spend, or receive today?

REFRAME

Your money story is not a life sentence — it's a *starting point.*

Every belief that once protected you can be rewritten to empower you.

You are not bound by the version of you who thought she had to "earn" love, success, or ease.
You are allowed to live a new story.

EMBODIMENT STEP

Take a deep breath.
Imagine your younger self sitting across from you — the version of you who first learned fear, guilt, or limitation around money.
Look her in the eyes and say:

"You did the best you could with what you knew.
But now, I lead our story differently."

Breathe deeply and visualize yourself writing a new money story — one filled with confidence, overflow, and trust.

Exercise Three

Releasing the Old Story

Take a deep breath.

On a new page, write down the money story that has defined you so far — the one rooted in scarcity, guilt, or fear.

Read it once.

Then say aloud:

"This story has taught me, but it no longer defines me."

Now, on the next page, write your new story — the one aligned with abundance, ease, and worthiness.

Old Story:

New Story:

JOURNAL PROMPTS

What would it look like to release the belief that "more" is dangerous?

How would I show up differently — in conversations, negotiations, and relationships — if *more* felt safe and natural?

What new story do I choose to write instead?

AFFIRMATION

I am rewriting my story.
I am a woman who receives abundantly because I know my worth.

EMBODIMENT STEP

Anchor the New Narrative

Over the next seven days, practice one simple act that reinforces your new story of abundance:

- Speak up about what you need.
- Charge your worth.
- Say yes to receiving help.
- Buy something that affirms your value, not your scarcity.

Each small act tells your subconscious:

"This is who I am now."

SECTION 4 CLOSING

You've faced your story, reclaimed your truth, and written a new chapter — one that aligns with abundance and self-trust.

You are no longer reacting to old programming; you are consciously creating your reality.

In the next section, we'll go deeper — into the emotional layers beneath your story — and begin *healing the wounds* that shaped it.

Section Five

LIMITING BELIEFS

LIMITING BELIEFS

The Invisible Ceiling

Your beliefs are the architecture of your reality.
They decide what's possible, what's probable, and what you unconsciously reject — even when you say you want it.

Most people try to change their circumstances without changing the beliefs that created them. That's like repainting a cracked wall without fixing the foundation.

Money doesn't respond to what you say you want.
It responds to what you *believe* you deserve.

These beliefs live deep within the subconscious — inherited through family, culture, and experience. They run quietly in the background, shaping every financial decision, often without you realizing it. They are the invisible ceilings that limit how high you allow yourself to rise.

The Anatomy of a Limiting Belief

A limiting belief is a subconscious rule your mind created to keep you safe. It usually begins as protection — not punishment. But over time, it becomes a ceiling you keep bumping into.

Common examples:

- "I have to work hard to earn money."
- "I'm bad with money."
- "If I make too much, people will resent me."
- "Money changes people."
- "Wanting more makes me greedy."
- "It's safer to stay small than to risk failing."

These beliefs run quietly in the background, influencing every decision — how you spend, what you charge, how you negotiate, and what you're willing to receive.

Exercise One

Identify Your Money Beliefs

Take a deep breath.
Without overthinking, complete the following sentences:

1. **Money is** ______________________________________
2. **Wealthy people are** ______________________________
3. **People like me have to** ___________________________
4. **If I had more money, I would** ______________________
5. **Wanting more means** _____________________________
6. **It's not safe to** ___________________________________

Now look at your answers.

Each statement reveals an energetic "rule" your subconscious is following.

Notice which ones feel heavy, constricting, or untrue — those are the ones ready to be rewritten.

Exercise Two

Reframe the Belief

Pick one limiting belief that feels the loudest.
Now, rewrite your new empowering belief in your own words.

Example:

Old: "I have to overwork to earn more."
New: "I earn more by aligning my energy, value, and purpose."

Write your new belief here:

Exercise Three

Collect the Evidence

Your mind loves proof. So give it some.

For your new belief, list three pieces of evidence — real or imagined — that it's possible.

Example:

- I've been paid easily for something I enjoyed.
- I know people who earn with ease and integrity.
- When I trust myself, opportunities appear.

Now list yours:

1. ____

2. ____

3. ____

The more evidence you gather, the more your nervous system believes.

JOURNAL PROMPTS

What beliefs have quietly dictated my financial limits?

What beliefs served me once (for safety or belonging) but no longer fit the woman I am now?

What would be possible if I believed money was safe, available, and abundant?

How would I act differently if I fully trusted this new belief?

MICRO-RITUAL

Thought to Truth

Whenever a limiting thought arises ("I can't," "It's too hard," "It'll never work"), pause and ask:

"Is this a fact, or a fear?"

Then say aloud:

"I choose a higher truth."

This simple interruption begins rewiring your neural and energetic pathways.

EMBODIMENT STEP

Acting "As If"

Pick one area of your financial life (asking, earning, receiving, spending). For the next 24 hours, behave *as if* your new belief were already true.

- If your new belief is "Money flows easily to me," act with calm confidence.
- If it's "I am safe to be visible and well-paid," post your offer, share your win, or send that invoice unapologetically.

Small, aligned actions signal your subconscious that the new story is real.

THE BELIEF AUDIT

From Limitation to Liberation

Your beliefs are energetic contracts.

Some still serve you. Others quietly sabotage your abundance. This worksheet helps you identify, release, and replace the ones that no longer align with the woman you're becoming.

Take your time. Be honest. Don't edit — awareness alone begins the healing.

Step 1 — Identify

Write down the *limiting beliefs* that currently shape your financial reality.

Think of phrases you catch yourself saying (or thinking) about money, work, or worth.

Examples:

- "I have to work hard to earn more."
- "I'm not great with money."
- "People won't pay me that much."
- "Money runs out fast."

Step 2 — Rewrite

For each belief, write a *new empowering truth* that expands you instead of contracts you.

Example:

- "I earn abundantly through alignment, not exhaustion."
- "I am capable, grounded, and trustworthy with money."
- "People are excited to pay me for the value I bring."
- "Money replenishes and multiplies easily."

Step 3 — Reinforce

Gather *daily proof* for your new belief.

This could be something small — a compliment, a client payment, a new opportunity, or even a sense of calm when spending.

Every piece of evidence tells your subconscious: *See? This is real now.*

Old Belief

New Truth

Daily Proof

REFLECTION PROMPT

Which new belief feels the most *true* in your body right now — even if just 2%?

What small action can you take today to embody it?

AFFIRMATION

I release the beliefs that limit my expansion.
I choose thoughts that support my abundance, safety, and power.
My beliefs create my reality — and I am choosing freedom.

SECTION 5 CLOSING

Your beliefs are the filters through which abundance flows.
When you upgrade the filter, you expand the flow.

You don't need to work harder to change your reality — you need to *believe differently.*

Every time you question an old belief, you reclaim power that was once hidden beneath it.

And every new belief you adopt becomes a building block in the foundation of your new wealth identity.

Section Six

HEALING MONEY WOUNDS

HEALING MONEY WOUNDS

Money wounds are emotional, energetic imprints formed from past experiences. They're left behind by moments when your nervous system felt unsafe around the topic of money — often during childhood and reinforced throughout life.

As an adult, these wounds live in your body, not your wallet. They're embedded in your subconscious and wired into your nervous system.

They aren't logical — but they are powerful, because they drive behavior on a subconscious level that you probably aren't even aware of.

They often create feelings of guilt, shame, fear, or scarcity around money. They don't reflect your earning potential, but they *do* shape your behaviors — how you earn, ask, receive, and spend. They make abundance feel out of reach, even when it's right in front of you.

They often whisper stories like:

- "I'm not good with money."
- "I'll lose it if I get it."
- "I don't deserve that much."
- "It's selfish to want more."

Healing your money wounds allows you to feel safe — no matter what your financial situation looks like. You'll know the wound is healing when no amount of money you have or make can disturb your inner sense of peace.

Exercise One

Name Your Wound

Each of us carries one or more **money wounds.**
They usually fall into one of these energetic themes:

1. **The Safety Wound** — "If I have too much, something bad will happen."

2. **The Worthiness Wound** — "I'm not valuable enough to be paid that."

3. **The Abandonment Wound** — "If I ask for more, they'll reject or replace me."

4. **The Guilt Wound** — "Others have it worse, who am I to want more?"

5. **The Control Wound** — "I can't trust others (or myself) with money."

Read through them.

Circle or star the one that feels most familiar in your body—where you feel a tightening, heat, or sting.

Now journal:

Which money wound feels most alive for me right now and how does it show up in my life or work?

Exercise Two

Trace It Back

Every wound has an origin point—a moment where safety or worth was first questioned.

Ask yourself:

1. When was the first time I felt unsafe, unworthy, or ashamed about money?
2. What was happening in that moment?
3. Who was involved, and what message did I receive?

Write it here without judgment. This isn't about blame—it's about awareness.

How has this experience made me feel about money?

Exercise Three

Reparent the Wound

Your inner child learned those beliefs to survive.
But you — the adult, the powerful woman — get to rewrite them.

Close your eyes.
Picture your younger self — the version of you who first felt that fear.
What does she need to hear right now?

Write her a letter:

"Dear (your name),
You did nothing wrong.
You were learning how to stay safe in a world that didn't yet feel safe.
But I've got you now.
You are safe, you are loved, and you are worthy of all that you desire."

Finish your letter here:

Read it out loud.
Your nervous system listens when you speak love to it.

JOURNAL PROMPTS

What emotion do I feel most often when I talk or think about money?

How have these emotions shaped my relationship with earning, saving, or spending?

What does safety with money feel like in my body?

EMBODIMENT STEP

Find a quiet space.
Place one hand on your heart, one on your lower belly.

Say softly:

"The version of me who learned fear about money did nothing wrong. She was surviving. I now lead with safety, worth and choice."

Visualize light moving through your body — clearing old fear, guilt, or shame. See that energy transform into gold — pure, radiant, limitless.

That gold is your new frequency: self-trust, safety, and sufficiency.

Visualize light moving through your body — clearing the old fear, guilt, or shame.

AFFIRMATION

I am no longer ruled by my money wounds. I am guided by self-trust, worth, and possibility.

SECTION 6 CLOSING

Money wounds run deep, but they can be healed.

They are messages from your younger self, asking for safety, not scarcity.

When you meet those parts of you with compassion, the wound becomes wisdom — and from that wisdom, you earn, receive, and create from power rather than pain.

Healing is not a single event nor is it linear. It's a process — layer by layer, memory by memory. You may uncover buried emotions or forgotten moments, each asking to be released.

Think of yourself as an onion, peeling back layers. With each layer, you uncover another memory or trauma ready to be healed and released before you can move to the next.

This takes time. Don't rush the process. Healing unfolds in its own divine timing and only when you're ready to face it.

Your willingness to face these patterns signals to your body that you are ready to surrender — because you finally feel safe enough to let go.

Release.
Heal.
Rise.

Section Seven

SHAME, GUILT AND THE FEMALE FINANCIAL WOUND

SHAME, GUILT AND THE FEMALE FINANCIAL WOUND

> "My mother, God rest her soul grew up in a time when a women's opinion didn't really matter. She, like most women played her role as wife and mother dutifully. She never stepped out or overstepped, and she certainly never complained. She just kept plugging away thanklessly and continued to run our household like a well-oiled machine. Until one day, she died—and the machine fell apart."

I wrote those words in my first book back in 2017. My mother was a teenager in the 1950s — and even though we're now a quarter century into the 2000s, those societal norms are far from extinct.

While women's roles have evolved, the *expectations* haven't disappeared. They're still woven into our culture — and, thanks to social media, they've intensified.

Today, women face an even heavier burden of perfection.

We believe breaking these "rules" damages our likability factor — and we feel that silent pressure to stay agreeable, accommodating and humble, even when it comes at a personal cost.

This creates a subtle cultural bias: An unspoken expectation that women should work tirelessly, dutifully, and without complaint just as my mother did.

At the root of this conditioning lie two powerful forces: **guilt** and **shame.**

- **Guilt** says: "I did something bad."
- **Shame** says: "I am bad."

Note the distinction.

Guilt can be resolved through apology, forgiveness, and repair. Shame, however, burrows into identity. It's more corrosive than guilt because it attacks the very part of us that believes we *can* change.

Shame disconnects us from our worth and separates our wholeness. It makes us desperate for validation and fearful of vulnerability.

This is the **female financial wound** — an inherited belief system that links a woman's worth to her sacrifice. It tells us it's noble to struggle, that "good women" don't care about money, and that comfort must be earned through suffering.

But this wound can only be healed through empathy — because shame cannot survive in the presence of compassion. Grace, understanding, and self-forgiveness are the medicine that transforms guilt into growth and shame into self-trust.

Exercise One

Identify Guilt or Shame

Close your eyes. Think of a recent money moment that still "stings." Notice where it lands.

- **Good-girl conditioning:** Be agreeable, grateful, low-maintenance.
- **Survivor's guilt:** Earning "more than my family ever did."
- **Receiving guilt:** Charging for your gifts or raising prices.
- **Debt shame:** Avoiding accounts or bills to escape the feeling.
- **Success shame:** Dimming your wins to stay likable.

Now, write what came up:

Exercise Two

The Guilt & Shame Inventory
→ The Repair Plan

Step 1— Name it (facts only).

What specific action or inaction around money triggers guilt?

Step 2 — Extract the lesson.

What value did I violate (e.g., honesty, timeliness, responsibility)?

Step 3 — Design the repair.

One tangible step I can take within 7 days:

Step 4 — Close the loop.

A sentence I'll say after completing the repair:

"I move forward with integrity."

Exercise Three

Release the Shame

Bring to mind the last time you felt guilt or embarrassment about money. Maybe you felt uncomfortable charging your worth, or you dimmed your success to make others comfortable.

Write that story here:

Then ask:

- What did I make that moment mean about me?
- What's the truth?

Say aloud:

"I release the shame that was never mine to carry."

Take a deep breath.
Visualize the shame lifting from your body like smoke turning into light.

Exercise Four

Releasing Inherited Shame

Complete these sentences:

- The first time I remember feeling money shame was when…

- The message I absorbed about me was…

- The truth I choose now is…

Note: Shame thrives in secrecy. Truth dissolves it.

The Cost of Carrying Shame

Where has money shame kept me silent, small, or stuck (undercharging, overspending, hiding)?

Receiving Without Guilt

What would it look like to receive generously — payment, praise, support — without apology?

Success Without Dimming

What would it look like to receive generously — payment, praise, support — without apology?

If My Best Friend Wrote This

What would I tell a friend who felt this same guilt or shame?

Exercise Five

Reclaim Your Permission

Write a list of desires that make you feel guilty — the ones you've labeled "too much" or "too selfish."

My forbidden desires:

1. ______________________________

2. ______________________________

3. ______________________________

4. ______________________________

5. ______________________________

Now look at each one and say aloud because saying them out loud helps to dissolve the shame:

"This desire is divine. It was planted in me for a reason."

You are not greedy for wanting more.
You are remembering your nature: expansion.

EMBODIMENT STEP

The Feminine Forgiveness Practice

Find a mirror.
Look into your own eyes — not critically, but compassionately.

Say softly:

"I forgive myself for every time I made myself small to be loved.
I forgive myself for confusing humility with limitation.
I forgive myself for believing my desires were too much."

Then smile — a gentle, knowing smile — and affirm:

"I am allowed to have more. I am allowed to receive."

Hold that gaze until you *feel* the truth settle in your body.

AFFIRMATION

I release shame and guilt around money.
My wealth is an act of self-love — and a gift to the world.

MICRO-RITUAL

The Self-Forgiveness Script

Hand on heart. Slow exhale.

"I forgive the past version of me who didn't know what I know now. She was surviving. I honor her. Today, I choose integrity, clarity, and self-trust."

Write one sentence to yourself now:

____

____

____

____

____

SECTION 7 CLOSING

You were never meant to apologize for your success.

As you release guilt and shame, you open the channel to your feminine receiving energy — the energy of ease, flow, and grace.

This isn't about taking from others.

It's about remembering that your abundance multiplies blessings for everyone.

When you rise, the world rises with you.

Section Eight

THE POWER OF FORGIVENESS

THE POWER OF FORGIVENESS:

Releasing the Past to Reclaim Your Power

Forgiveness isn't about excusing what happened.
It's about setting yourself free.

Holding onto resentment keeps you tied to the very energy you're trying to escape. It keeps you looping in the past — replaying the story, reliving the pain, and reinforcing the wound.

When you forgive, you're not saying *it was okay.* You're saying, *I'm ready to stop letting it define me.*

Many of our money wounds are tangled up with other people — parents who struggled, bosses who underpaid us, partners who judged us, or friends who made us feel guilty for wanting more. But forgiveness isn't for them — it's for you.

Because every ounce of resentment you hold blocks your receiving energy.

Forgiveness creates energetic space for abundance to flow in.

When you release judgment — of others *and* yourself — you raise your frequency from contraction to expansion, from scarcity to peace.

True forgiveness is radical self-liberation.

It's reclaiming your power from the past.

It's closing old energetic contracts that keep you tied to stories of pain, lack or betrayal.

And most importantly, it's remembering:
You did the best you could with what you knew at the time.
And so did everyone else.

Exercise One

Forgiving Others

Think of at least one person whose actions — intentional or not — created pain around money, worth, or safety.

This might be:

- A parent who modeled scarcity.
- A boss who undervalued you.
- A partner who made you feel dependent.
- A friend who shamed your ambition.

Write their names here:

Now, complete these sentences:

- The story I've been telling myself about what happened is…

- The truth beneath the story is…

- What I wish they had known or said is…

Then, say this statement aloud: "I forgive you, not because you deserve it, but because I deserve peace."

That's your power returning to you.

Exercise Two

Forgiving Yourself

Self-forgiveness is the most radical act of self-love.

We often punish ourselves for past financial mistakes — the debt, the impulsive spending, the times we didn't speak up, or the moments we accepted less than we deserved.

But guilt keeps you tethered to an old identity.
Forgiveness invites your future self to take the lead.

I forgive myself for…

Now place your hand on your heart and say aloud:

"I forgive myself."
"I honor myself."
"I love myself."

Then, wrap your arms around yourself and give your body a gentle hug.

Rubbing your arms to comfort yourself soothes the nervous system. Doing this while repeating these phrases helps rewire your mind away from stress and self-judgment — and into love, safety, and peace.

Exercise Three

The Forgiveness Letter

Write a letter to someone (alive or not) whom you're ready to forgive — or to yourself.

You don't have to send it. The power lies in the writing.

"Dear ________,
You hurt me when ________.
For a long time, I believed ________.
But now I choose to see it differently.
I release the anger, the guilt, and the shame.
I no longer need this story to feel safe.
I am free. And so are you."

Read it once, then tear it up,
burn it safely, or bury it — symbolizing your release.

JOURNAL PROMPTS

Who in my life (including myself) am I still not ready to forgive — and why?

What would need to change in order for you to be ready to forgive them?

How does forgiveness make me feel?

EMBODIMENT STEP

The Heart Expansion Practice

Find a quiet space.
Sit comfortably. Place one hand on your heart and one on your lower belly.

Breathe in deeply.
On the exhale, whisper:

"I forgive. I release. I am free."

Visualize your heart expanding — soft golden light radiating outward.

Feel yourself becoming lighter with every breath.

This is forgiveness as energy work — a return to your natural vibration of love and abundance.

AFFIRMATION

I forgive the past.
I release the need to replay the pain.
I am free, whole, and open to receive.

SECTION 8 CLOSING

Forgiveness isn't forgetting. It's remembering without pain.

It's the moment your past loses its grip and your future starts breathing again.

When you forgive, you declare:
"My peace matters more than my proof."

And from that peace, abundance flows effortlessly.

Section Nine

REWRITING THE NARRATIVE

REWRITING THE NARRATIVE

You've done the hardest part — you've faced your story. You've uncovered the fears, patterns, and wounds that have quietly shaped your relationship with money.

Now, it's time to rewrite the narrative.

You are not your past.

You are not your parents' beliefs.

You are not your salary history, your job title, or your bank balance. You are the author of your next chapter — and that chapter begins with a decision.

Every time you choose self-worth over self-doubt, you are writing a new page.

Every time you speak up, charge your value, or receive with gratitude instead of guilt, you are shifting generations of programming. Every "yes" to your worth is a declaration that the cycle ends with you.

Rewriting isn't about pretending the past never happened.

It's about honoring it for the wisdom it gave you — and choosing to lead differently from here.

You can't create a new story while clinging to the old one.

So today, we let the old narrative rest.

And we begin to write the truth — your truth — of abundance, worthiness, and self-trust.

Exercise One

Belief Audit

Your story is written through your beliefs — and beliefs can be rewritten at any time.

Take inventory of what you've been telling yourself about money, power, and possibility.

Limiting Belief	Where It Came From	New Empowered Belief
"Money is hard to make."	Dad's struggle with work.	"Money flows easily when I align with purpose."
"I'm bad with money."	Childhood mistakes or shame.	"I'm learning and improving every day."
"Rich people are greedy."	Family conditioning.	"Wealth amplifies good intentions."

Now complete your own list below:

Exercise Two

Visualizing the Rewrite

Close your eyes.
Imagine the version of you who lives this new story fully.

She's calm when she checks her accounts.
She speaks about money with confidence and ease.
She gives and receives without apology.
She trusts herself.

What does she wear?
How does she move?
How does she carry herself?
What kind of decisions does she make?

Now say to yourself:

"I am her. She is me. We are one."

VISUALIZATION

The Abundant Self

Close your eyes and imagine the version of you who lives this new story fully.

She's calm when she checks her accounts.
She negotiates with ease.
She gives and receives freely.
She trusts herself.

What does she wear?
How does she speak?
How does she carry herself?
What does her life look and feel like?

Now, say to yourself:

"I am her. She is me. We are one."

JOURNAL PROMPTS

Let's expand on your new story. Visualize the identity you want to become and begin to embody her.

MICRO-PRACTICE

The Daily Rewrite

Each morning, before you reach for your phone or open your laptop, write one sentence beginning with:

"My new story is…"

For example:

- "My new story is that wealth flows to me through ease and joy."
- "My new story is that I am fully supported in every decision I make."
- "My new story is that I no longer chase — I attract."

Speak it out loud.
Feel it in your body.
Your nervous system learns through repetition — every word you affirm becomes a command to the universe.

SECTION 9 CLOSING

You've done the inner work — the healing, the remembering, the rewriting.
From here, your relationship with money becomes less about control and more about **co-creation.**

You are no longer the woman who settles.
You are the woman who *chooses.*
You are no longer chasing abundance.
You *embody* it.

Your power lies not in what you earn, but in how you see yourself — and now, you see clearly.

Section Ten

I AM ENOUGH

I AM ENOUGH

There's a moment in every woman's journey when she realizes that the chase — for money, approval, or validation — was never about having more.

It was about feeling *enough.*

Self-worth is not earned.

It's remembered. Reclaimed. Re-rooted in truth.

It is the belief in your value, your contribution, and your right to ask for more.

You were born enough — but conditioned to believe otherwise.

The world taught you that "enough" lives somewhere outside of you — in a number, a title, a compliment, a partner, or a bank balance.

But "enough" isn't earned. It's remembered.

When you operate from enoughness, you stop negotiating for scraps and start expecting alignment.

You stop apologizing for your needs and start honoring your value.

You stop chasing validation and start magnetizing opportunity.

"I am enough" isn't just an affirmation — it's a frequency.

It's the vibration that magnetizes abundance, ease, and self-trust.

When you feel "enough," you stop hustling for worth and begin embodying it.

You stop proving and start *being*.

Exercise One

The Enoughness Inventory

Close your eyes and place one hand on your heart. Think of all the ways you've tried to prove your worth — through overworking, over-giving, over-achieving, or over-pleasing.

Then, on paper, finish these sentences:

- I've tried to earn my worth by…

- I feel like I'm "not enough" when…

- The truth is…

Pause.
You don't have to earn your worth anymore.

Exercise Two

The "I Am Enough" Mirror Practice

Stand before a mirror.
Look directly into your own eyes — not at your hair, not at your clothes — at **you.**

Say slowly:

"I am enough. I have always been enough. I will always be enough."

Notice what emotions surface — disbelief, tears, laughter, resistance. Each time you repeat these words, you rewire your nervous system to recognize your natural worth.

Write what comes up for you here:

JOURNAL PROMPTS

Where in my life do I still feel like I have something to prove?

When did I first believe I wasn't enough — and who taught me that?

How would I show up differently if I deeply knew that I was already enough?

How does it feel in my body when I say "I am enough"?

EMBODIMENT STEP

The Anchor of Enough

For the next 24 hours, notice every moment you feel the urge to justify, explain, or overperform.
Each time, pause and place your hand on your heart.
Say silently:

"I am enough."

Feel your body soften.
Let that be your new baseline of being.

AFFIRMATION

I am enough.

I have always been enough.

I will always be enough.

SECTION 10 CLOSING

You no longer have to strive to *become* more to be worthy of abundance.
You already are abundance — the source, not the seeker.

From this place of wholeness, everything you desire begins to flow with ease.

You are not chasing validation; you are embodying value.
You are enough — exactly as you are, in this very moment.

Section Eleven

POWER, PERMISSION AND THE DIVINE FEMININE

POWER, PERMISSION AND THE DIVINE FEMININE

For centuries, women were taught to wait for permission — to speak, to act, to lead, to want. But permission never comes from the system that benefits from your silence.

Power has many faces.

For men, it has often looked like assertion, control, logic, and direction — the energy of *doing*.

For women, true power flows through intuition, magnetism, creation, and compassion — the energy of *being*.

We each carry both the masculine and the feminine within us.

The masculine drives action, structure, and focus.

The feminine leads with intuition, empathy, and flow.

The Divine Feminine doesn't chase. She attracts.

She doesn't grasp. She receives.

She doesn't shout. She embodies.

Yet many of us have internalized the masculine model of power — performative, logical, and outcome-driven — while suppressing the intuitive, creative, receptive qualities that are equally vital.

When you reject the feminine within you, you disconnect from your natural flow — your ability to manifest, to magnetize, to move through life with grace and certainty.

Stepping into your divine feminine energy is not about rejecting the masculine.

It's about integrating the two — action and intuition, structure and flow, logic and faith.

Power balanced with softness. Drive anchored in presence.

When these energies harmonize, you no longer seek permission.

You *are* the permission.

You move differently. You speak differently.

You carry an energy that commands respect — not through force, but through embodiment.

Exercise One

Power Reclaimed

Reflect on a time when you gave away your power — maybe by staying silent, dimming your light, or waiting for validation.

Write about it briefly, without judgment:

Now ask yourself:

What would I have said or done if I had trusted my power in that moment?

Then finish this sentence:

"Next time, I will honor my truth by..."

Exercise Two

Feminine vs. Masculine Power

Divide your page into two columns.

On the left, write: **Masculine Power**
On the right, write: **Feminine Power**

List the traits or behaviors you associate with each.

Example:

Masculine Power	**Feminine Power**
Action	Intuition
Logic	Creativity
Force	Flow
Control	Surrender
Direction	Expansion

Now reflect:

Where am I over-relying on one energy?
Where can I invite more balance?

Write your insights:

JOURNAL PROMPTS

Where in my life do I still wait for permission — to ask, to lead, to receive?

What does "feminine power" feel like in my body?

How would my life change if I stopped seeking validation and started trusting my energy?

What does integrating both my masculine and feminine energy look like in my daily life?

EMBODIMENT STEP

The Receiving Practice

For one full day, practice the art of *receiving.*
Compliments, help, gifts, ideas — whatever comes your way.
Say only two words in response:

"Thank you."

No deflecting. No diminishing. No "you didn't have to."
Let yourself feel what it's like to *receive without guilt.*

AFFIRMATION

I no longer wait for permission.
I *am* the permission.
My power flows from within — balanced, grounded, divine.

SECTION 11 CLOSING

Feminine power is quiet but unshakable.
It doesn't demand attention — it commands it.
You don't have to prove your power or perform your worth.
You only have to remember who you are.

When you embody your divine feminine energy, you become the permission slip you've been waiting for — and everything you desire begins to flow toward you effortlessly.

Section Twelve

CULTIVATING AN ABUNDANT STATE OF BEING

CULTIVATING AN ABUNDANT STATE OF BEING

Abundance isn't something you chase.

It's something you *become.*

You don't attract what you want — you attract what you *are.*

You don't manifest from hustle or control. You manifest from alignment.

When you live in a state of *becoming,* you embody the future you desire before it arrives.

You think, feel, and act as the woman who already has it.

Energy doesn't lie.

When your internal world radiates gratitude, worthiness, and confidence, your external world rearranges to meet it.

This is how abundance flows:

From being → to belief → to becoming → to having.

Your work now is not to *force* results, but to *stabilize* your state — to hold the vibration of abundance even before it's visible.

Exercise One

Embodying the Future Self

Close your eyes.
Imagine the version of you who already lives in abundance.
She's not striving — she's steady.
She's not chasing — she's attracting.
She's not waiting — she's walking in it.

Ask yourself:

- What does her morning feel like?
- How does she speak?
- What decisions does she make with ease?
- What boundaries protect her peace?
- What does she no longer tolerate?

Write your answers below:

Now, take one small aligned action today that your abundant self would take naturally.
Just one.

Exercise Two

Frequency Rehearsal

Throughout your day, pause three times.
Ask yourself:
"Am I operating from scarcity or sufficiency?"
If scarcity, take one deep breath, place a hand on your heart, and repeat softly:

"I am safe. I am supported. I am enough."

Feel your body soften.
That's you shifting into alignment.

EMBODIMENT PRACTICE

The Coffee Exercise

Go to a luxury hotel or café — somewhere that feels slightly outside your comfort zone.

Order one cup of coffee, tea, or dessert.
Sit tall, breathe deeply, and simply *be* there.
You belong in beautiful spaces.

This practice trains your nervous system to feel safe in environments of abundance.

When you leave, write how it felt:

JOURNAL PROMPTS

What emotions come up when I imagine already living in abundance?

What actions, habits, or thoughts would my future abundant self no longer engage in?

What would I do differently if I fully trusted that abundance was inevitable?

What daily rituals keep me grounded in gratitude, confidence, and flow?

AFFIRMATION

I am no longer becoming — I *am.*
I move through life with ease, confidence, and grace.
Abundance is not what I chase — it's what I embody.

SECTION 12 CLOSING

Becoming isn't about doing more — it's about *remembering more.* The more you remember who you are, the more the world mirrors that truth back to you.

Abundance isn't something outside of you — it's something that flows *through* you.
Every moment of presence, gratitude, and belief draws it closer until it simply *is.*

You are already her.
Now live like it.

Section Thirteen

STEPPING INTO YOUR ABUNDANCE FREQUENCY

STEPPING INTO YOUR ABUNDANCE FREQUENCY

Every frequency holds a story.
Scarcity tells you there's not enough.
Abundance tells you there's more than you could ever need.

You've done the inner work — you've named your wounds, released shame, rewritten the narrative, and remembered your worth.
Now it's time to *embody* that new frequency — to step into the energetic signature of a woman who already has what she desires.

Your abundance frequency isn't created through force.
It's accessed through *alignment.*

It begins with how you feel — not what you do.
You can't manifest abundance from the vibration of fear, guilt, or lack.
You must become the energetic match for what you seek.

You don't attract what you want.

You attract what you *are.*

When you tune your energy to abundance, everything around you begins to reorganize to match it.

You'll notice coincidences, synchronicities, new opportunities — not by accident, but by resonance.

Exercise One

Calibrating to Abundance

Sit quietly and take three deep breaths.
Place your hand on your heart and ask yourself:

"What does abundance feel like in my body?"

Don't overthink it — just sense it.
Is it warmth?
Lightness?
A gentle expansion in your chest?
Peace in your belly?

Write what you feel:

Now, amplify that feeling.
Imagine dialing it up — as if you're turning the volume of abundance from 3 to 10.

Hold that energy for one full minute.
That's your frequency calibration.
You just shifted your vibration.

Exercise Two

Anchoring the Frequency

Choose one small ritual to embody your abundance daily.
It could be lighting a candle before work, wearing perfume that makes you feel luxurious, taking a longer shower, or saying your affirmations while you dress.

The ritual doesn't create the abundance — *you do.*
The ritual simply reminds your nervous system that you already live in abundance now.

Describe your ritual here:

Exercise Three

The Luxury of Presence

Abundance is presence — the ability to fully experience this moment.

For one day, slow down.
Taste your food.
Feel the water on your skin.
Look people in the eye.
Speak slower.
Savor your life.

Then write:
What did I notice when I allowed myself to be fully present?

JOURNAL PROMPTS

What is my current energetic set point — scarcity, neutrality, or abundance?

What activities, environments, or people raise my vibration?

What habits or thoughts lower it?

What does my next-level abundance feel like emotionally — not just financially?

EMBODIMENT PRACTICE

The Frequency Walk

Put on music that makes you feel confident and expansive.
Walk — slowly, intentionally, powerfully.
Feel each step connect you deeper to your abundant self.

As you walk, repeat softly:

"I am abundance in motion."
"I am magnetic to wealth, love, and opportunity."

Your body learns through repetition.
The more you *move* like her, the faster you become her.

AFFIRMATION

I am aligned with the frequency of abundance.
I attract wealth, joy, and success by simply being who I am.

SECTION 13 CLOSING

Stepping into your abundance frequency is a daily choice.
It's not something you turn on and off — it's a way of being.

When you align your emotions, thoughts, and actions with abundance, the universe has no choice but to respond in kind.
Because energy never lies.

Keep calibrating.
Keep aligning.
Keep allowing.

You are the frequency.
And the world is tuning to *you.*

Section Fourteen

THE LAW OF ALLOWING

THE LAW OF ALLOWING

The Law of Allowing is one of the most powerful — and most misunderstood — universal laws.

It's not about doing more.

It's about *trusting more.*

Allowing is the art of releasing resistance — the fear, the control, the constant pushing.

It's learning to let go of the need to force outcomes and instead open yourself to receive what's already on its way.

You've been taught that effort equals worth.

That if you just work harder, try longer, and hustle more — *then* things will fall into place.

But effort without energetic alignment creates exhaustion, not expansion.

When you align with the Law of Allowing, you stop fighting against the flow of life.

You stop grasping.

You stop waiting.

You simply allow yourself to receive.

KEY TRUTH

Allowing doesn't mean inaction — it means aligned action.

It means trusting that once you've planted the seed, the soil knows what to do.

You don't stand over a seed and demand it to grow faster — you nurture it, trust it, and allow it to bloom in divine timing.

Money, opportunities, and abundance respond the same way.

Your job is not to chase them.

Your job is to *stay open* to receiving them.

Exercise One

Identifying Resistance

What are you currently trying to control?
Maybe it's a deadline, an outcome, a relationship, or the pace of your success.

Write them down here:

Now ask yourself:

"What would it feel like to trust that this is already working out in my favor?"

Notice the shift in your body when you move from control → to trust. That feeling is alignment.

Exercise Two

The Art of Surrender

For the next 24 hours, release one thing you've been forcing. It could be constantly checking your bank account, obsessing over a client response, or worrying about how money will come in.

Each time the urge arises, say softly to yourself:

"I trust the process. Everything is unfolding perfectly for me."

Observe how your energy changes when you choose trust over control.

JOURNAL PROMPTS

What areas of my life am I still trying to control out of fear or lack of trust?

How does my body feel when I'm in resistance versus when I'm in allowance?

What would it look like to relax into the belief that everything I desire is already on its way to me?

What would I do differently today if I *knew* abundance was inevitable?

EMBODIMENT PRACTICE

Floating in Flow

Find a quiet place to sit or lie down.

Close your eyes and imagine yourself floating on calm water.
You're not swimming or struggling — just floating, fully supported.
You feel held, weightless, and safe.

Now imagine that this water represents abundance — infinite, surrounding, and supporting you.
You don't need to chase it. You only need to *allow it.*

Breathe in trust.
Exhale control.
Repeat until your whole body softens.

AFFIRMATION

I release resistance.
I trust the timing of my life.
What is meant for me flows effortlessly into my experience.

SECTION 14 CLOSING

When you master the Law of Allowing, abundance becomes natural. You no longer have to "make things happen." You align, you trust, and you allow.

The universe always meets you halfway — but only when you stop standing in your own way. Surrender is not weakness. It's the ultimate act of confidence. You are safe to let life love you back.

Section Fifteen

GRATITUDE

GRATITUDE:

The Gateway to Abundance

Gratitude is the highest currency in the energetic economy of the universe. It multiplies everything it touches.

When you live in gratitude, you are saying to Life:

“I see the good. I receive it fully. I am ready for more.”

Gratitude doesn’t deny pain or pretend that everything is perfect — it simply shifts focus from what’s missing to what’s present. And in doing so, it raises your frequency to the vibration where abundance already exists.

Gratitude is the frequency of abundance. It is the bridge between where you are and where you’re going — the energetic portal that transforms scarcity into sufficiency and desire into manifestation.
When you live in gratitude, you train your nervous system to recognize safety, expansion, and joy. You tell the universe: *I am ready to receive more of this.*

Gratitude is not simply a polite "thank you." It's an emotional state — a vibration that activates the heart. It's the moment you pause and breathe in the fullness of what already exists.

Even in moments of uncertainty, gratitude grounds you in trust. Even in seasons of loss, it reminds you that something beautiful is still being born.

When you can hold gratitude for both the blessings and the lessons, you become magnetic to more good — not because you're performing thankfulness, but because you've aligned with the truth:
You already have enough.
You already *are* enough.

The Emotion of Gratitude

Gratitude isn't just a mindset — it's an *emotional frequency* that rewires the body.
When you feel genuine gratitude, your nervous system relaxes.
Your heart rhythm synchronizes.
Your mind softens.

Physiologically, gratitude floods your body with oxytocin and dopamine — the same chemicals associated with safety and love.
Energetically, it opens your receiving channels, signaling to the universe:

"I am full, whole, and open to more."
The emotion of gratitude bridges the gap between scarcity and sufficiency.
It transforms need into nourishment and fear into faith.

Exercise One

The Gratitude Frequency

Take three deep breaths.
Place your hand on your heart and close your eyes.

Think of one thing you are deeply grateful for — not from your mind, but from your soul.
Feel it in your body.

Notice the warmth that spreads in your chest, the softening in your shoulders, the calm in your breath.
That's the energy of receiving.

Write about it here:

Now, choose one thing you are grateful for that hasn't yet manifested. Thank it as if it's already yours.

"Thank you for this opportunity, this relationship, this abundance that's already on its way."

This is how you collapse time.
Gratitude draws the future into the present.

Exercise Two

The Emotional Alchemy of Gratitude

When you shift into gratitude, you're not ignoring reality — you're *alchemizing* it.
You're teaching your body that joy can coexist with uncertainty.

Reflect and write:

1. What recent challenge brought me unexpected wisdom or strength?

2. How did it ultimately serve my growth or expansion?

3. What can I thank that experience for now?

This practice dissolves resentment and turns pain into power.

Exercise Three

Daily Gratitude Expansion

For the next seven days, write down three things you're grateful for each morning — and three more each evening.

Try not to repeat any.

At the end of the week, read them all aloud.
You'll see evidence of how much abundance already surrounds you.

JOURNAL PROMPTS

What emotions arise when I practice gratitude — peace, joy, safety, relief?

How does gratitude shift the way I make financial or life decisions?

When do I forget to practice gratitude — and what does that reveal?

How can I make gratitude my default emotional state?

EMBODIMENT PRACTICE

The Gratitude Walk

Take a slow walk outside.
With each step, name something you're grateful for — silently or aloud.
Start with the simple: "I'm grateful for this breath. I'm grateful for this light. I'm grateful for this body that carries me."

By the end of your walk, notice how your energy has softened, expanded, and elevated.
That's your vibration shifting.

AFFIRMATION

I am surrounded by abundance.
Gratitude expands my capacity to receive.
The more I appreciate, the more I attract.

SECTION 15 CLOSING

Gratitude is the gateway to everything you desire.
It's the highest form of wealth — the one that multiplies simply by being felt.

When you live in gratitude, life becomes a mirror reflecting your appreciation back to you in greater measure.
This is how you stay in flow.
This is how you stay magnetic.

The woman who gives thanks for what she already has... will never live in lack again.

Section Sixteen

FINAL REFLECTIONS

FINAL REFLECTION

You Were Always Worthy

This journey wasn't about becoming someone new.
It was about remembering who you've always been.

You've peeled back the layers of conditioning, scarcity, and fear. You've faced your money wounds, rewritten your story, and reconnected to your worth. You've learned that abundance doesn't come from effort — it comes from embodiment. You've learned that wealth isn't something you chase — it's something you allow.

You've redefined success on your terms.
You've reclaimed your feminine power.
You've remembered that your value was never up for negotiation.

Every page you've written, every tear you've shed, every truth you've acknowledged has brought you closer to yourself — the woman beneath the armor, the one who trusts, receives, and shines.
As you step forward from this work, know this:
You are no longer the woman who doubts her power.
You are the woman who owns it.

JOURNAL PROMPT

A Letter to Your Future Self

Write a letter to your future self — one year from today.
Describe how your life has changed since you decided to claim your worth and live in alignment with abundance.

Who have you become?
What opportunities, relationships, and experiences have flowed to you with ease?
How does it feel to live as the woman who knows she's worthy of it all?

Start here:

"Dear Future Me,
I am so proud of you for..."

Revisit this one year from now and witness how much of it has already come true.

FINAL AFFIRMATION

I am the embodiment of abundance.
I am the author of my story.
I am the woman I once dreamed of becoming.
I was never broken — only becoming.
And I am finally home.

EPILOGUE

This isn't the end of your journey — it's your awakening.

You've remembered what was never lost:
Your power.
Your voice.
Your worth.

Carry this energy with you into every conversation, every choice, and every new chapter.

Because when a woman heals her relationship with money, she doesn't just change her life — she changes the world.

Congratulations on your achievement!

While this may be the end of the journal, it's just the beginning of your money transformation.

Now that you've stepped into a new version of yourself, greater abundance will naturally flow your way.

Keep going — the rewards are sweet, and you're standing at the precipice of absolute bliss.

Stay brilliant and shine,
xo,
Tamara

About the Author

Tamara Lashchyk is a former Wall Street executive turned career strategist and coach, with over 25 years of experience navigating the high-stakes world of global finance. After leaving the corporate arena, she founded TDL International—a company dedicated to helping professionals unlock their full potential.

Tamara's journey didn't begin with privilege. She grew up in a home where the lights were often shut off, credit cards were declined, and financial instability was a constant undercurrent. After the devastating loss of her mother, her father filed for bankruptcy—leaving Tamara with $50,000 in student loans (the equivalent of $118,000 today).

Despite landing an internship on Wall Street, a recession forced her to bag groceries after graduation just to make ends meet. Through perseverance, she eventually secured a position at J.P. Morgan—her dream firm—where she worked tirelessly to stand out. Yet even with outward success, the burden of debt and the emotional weight tied to money continued to haunt her.

Tamara carried deep-rooted scars from her upbringing, and it wasn't until she discovered personal development and the energetics of money that she began to heal. Along the way, she uncovered a powerful truth: financial freedom isn't just about money—it's about releasing the fear and shame we associate with it.

Today, Tamara empowers women to rewrite their financial stories. Through her coaching and her innovative *Empower Her Money* series, she helps women break free from scarcity thinking and step boldly into lives of abundance and purpose.